The motor narrowboat 'Comet' passes down the 'long pound' at Stoke Bruerne on the Grand Union Canal in 1985, while reconstructing a working trip.

Canal Narrowboats
and Barges

Tony Conder

Published in 2004 by Shire Publications Ltd,
Cromwell House, Church Street, Princes Risborough,
Buckinghamshire HP27 9AA, UK.
(Website: www.shirebooks.co.uk)

Copyright © 2004 by Tony Conder.
First published 2004.
Shire Album 427. ISBN 0 7478 0587 3.
Tony Conder is hereby identified as the author of this work
in accordance with Section 77 of the Copyright, Designs
and Patents Act 1988.

British Library Cataloguing in Publication Data:
Conder, Tony
Canal narrowboats and barges. – (Shire album; 427)
1. Canal-boats – Great Britain
2. Barges – Great Britain
3. Canals – Great Britain – History
I. Title
623.8'2436'0941
ISBN 0 7478 0587 3.

Front cover: *Narrowboats outside the Island Warehouse at Ellesmere Port, where the Boat Museum preserves the heritage of the working waterways.*

Back cover: *The author, Tony Conder, steers the Leeds-Liverpool Canal short boat 'Kennet' down Wigan locks for dry-docking at Worsley.*

ACKNOWLEDGEMENTS
This book would not have been possible without the assistance of individuals, clubs and
societies nationwide, many of which are mentioned in the text or the further information
sections at the back of the book. Particular thanks are due to David McDougall for
access to his collection and for his advice and encouragement, to Tony Lewery and Mike
Clarke for their support and advice over many years, to Marilyn McDougall for
technical and scanning expertise with the photographs, to Judy Wootton for translating
the written word to the word processor and to Angela Conder for sharing the driving,
for proof reading and for being able to spell.
Photographs are acknowledged as follows: David Blagrove, pages 4, 5
(bottom), 48 (all), 49 (top); Tony Lewery, pages 30, 31 (top), 33 (top and centre), 49
(bottom), 51 (all), 52 (both); David McDougall Collection, pages 3, 6 (both), 7 (centre), 9
(bottom), 11 (centre), 12, 14 (top), 17 (both), 18 (centre), 19 (both), 20 (top), 21 (both), 22
(top and bottom), 24 (both), 25 (top), 26 (bottom), 28 (bottom), 32 (top), 33 (bottom), 34
(bottom), 35 (both), 36, 37 (both), 39 (both), 40, 41 (both), 42 (all), 43 (both), 44 (both), 50
(top); Robin Smithett/Sight Seen Partnership, pages 23 (all), 34 (top), 55; Roger Wickson,
pages 28 (top), 45 (all), 46. All other photographs are the author's own.

Printed in Malta by Gutenberg Press Limited, Gudja Road,
Tarxien PLA 19, Malta.

Contents

The narrowboat 'Northwich' arrives for loading at Preston Brook, Cheshire, c.1910.

Introduction

Canals in Britain are more popular with the public today than they have ever been. When you walk the towpath, take holidays on a canal boat or visit events you will see boats of all shapes and sizes; this book will help you identify the major types and understand their history.

There are still many of the older iron, steel and wooden working boats on the inland waterways. Used until the 1970s to carry all types of cargoes for factories and works, most have now been consigned to leisure use. It is, however, still possible to see loaded working narrowboats as enthusiasts keep trade going. These vessels mostly carry coal but also experiment with other cargoes in an attempt to win back canal trade from the roads and railways. There are also generations of new boats built for the leisure market that carry on some of the traditions of the narrowboat.

On broad waterways barges do still work commercially but many types are preserved as houseboats or for leisure use. A small number of preserved sailing barges help recapture the great trading days on the rivers and estuaries.

Narrowboats 'Archimedes' and 'Fazeley' pass south through Soulbury Locks on the Grand Union Canal with fence panels in 1994.

A spritsail barge approaches Maldon on the River Blackwater in 1998.

Narrowboat 'Clover' progresses north through Middlewich on the Trent & Mersey Canal in 1999, passing boats loaded with salt.

The typical shape of a river barge, wide and shallow-draughted. This is a Chelmer & Blackwater Navigation barge at Heybridge, c.1900.

Broad and narrow waterways

Around 4000 miles (6400 km) of improved rivers and canals have been built in Britain and most of these are still in use. About one-third of waterways were built 'narrow' – meaning with locks measuring 70 feet (21.34 metres) by 7 feet (2.13 metres).

Individuals, companies and groups of shareholders built up the canal and river systems in short lengths. Locks on rivers were built to the size appropriate to their depth and flow and the early canals followed these sizes. Lock lengths vary from 60 feet (18.28

A small Yorkshire barge on the Huddersfield Broad Canal, c.1910.

A chalk-carrying barge from the River Arun preserved at the Boat Museum, Ellesmere Port.

metres) on the older Yorkshire waterways to 600 feet (182.88 metres) on the Manchester Ship Canal.

Barges on broad canals vary in size, shape and style because they originated from many local roots. Often their design was influenced by previous traditions of shipbuilding. On the east coast of England boats were built in the Viking tradition with overlapping wooden planks ('clinker') and large square sails – typified by the sailing keel of the Humber estuary. In the south, smooth sides with the planks lying beside one another ('carvel') and a more fore-and-aft rig were typical of southern European shipbuilding.

The first Act of Parliament authorising a river improvement was passed for the River Lee in 1424. There was another burst of work before

Left: *A square-sailed keel on the Yorkshire waterways, c.1900.*

The carvel bows of a River Wey Navigation barge, one of the family of boats related to the spritsail barges of the Thames estuary.

and after the English Civil War in the 1640s and 1650s, and then
steady progress took place all round Britain from 1700 onwards.
Schemes were often simple, involving the connection of an
inland town to the sea or to a supply of raw materials for
industry.

When narrow canals began to be built in the 1760s many
linked mines to factories and towns over short distances; very few
canals were built with a national network in mind. The exception
to this is the 'cross' of waterways formed by the Trent & Mersey
Canal, the Staffordshire & Worcestershire Canal and the
Coventry and Oxford Canals, linking England's four major
estuaries: the Severn, the Thames, the Humber and the Mersey.

There were instances of broad boats influencing narrowboat
design or of the same navigation factors being taken into account
for the two types of boat. The large narrowboats of the River

*A Leeds–Liverpool Canal short
boat, 'George', with the typical
transom stern of the earlier-built
boats at the Boat Museum.*

*'Bacup', one of the later-built
Leeds–Liverpool Canal motor
short boats at the Boat Museum.*

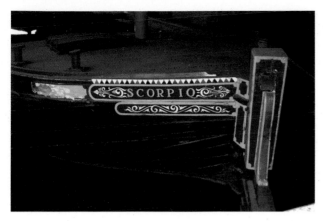

'Scorpio', one of the long boats built for the Liverpool end of the Leeds–Liverpool Canal, at the Boat Museum.

Severn and the barge-style boats of the Chesterfield Canal and River Trent are examples.

One of the most complex boat-building histories is that of the Leeds–Liverpool Canal, where lock lengths were different at either end of the waterway and the northern and southern traditions of boat-building met.

Among the great fleets of trading boats were other working craft: victualling boats on the estuaries taking food, water and other supplies to seagoing craft; official boats such as inspection and engineers' mobile offices; ferries; passenger craft; and maintenance boats. All took their shape from the local waterway.

Modern craft have filled the space left by their trading predecessors. A holiday narrowboat may be known as a 'trad', with the high hull sides of the narrowboat travelling empty. 'Tugs' have hulls with little freeboard and often have only portholes, not windows, in the superstructure. These boats now have their own place in canal history, where leisure has been the dominant factor since the 1950s.

Mersey flats supplying seagoing ships in Birkenhead Docks, c.1910.

The only surviving flat, 'Mossdale', in the Boat Museum collection.

Barges

The fundamental barge types on the inland waterways in England are linked to the four major rivers and their estuaries.

In the north-west there was the *Mersey flat* and its variations. The sailing and coasting flats developed unpowered or 'dumb' varieties for the local waterways. The River Severn had large, simple sailing boats, the *trows*, which varied in size and style from small upriver craft to larger seagoing boats that sailed all around the south-west peninsula. *Spritsail barges* kept London supplied with food and raw materials for its industries from the east coast and smaller barges with similar hulls worked on the Thames and its tributaries. *Keels*, with their large square sails, typified the north-east. Each river and canal that joined the Humber had its own size of boat to fit the local locks and bridges.

In Scotland, sailing *gabbarts* gave their hull shape to a range of steam, and later diesel, 'puffers'. Some worked on the canals; larger boats served the Highlands and Islands.

The trow 'Spry' in dry dock at Gloucester during a brief period when she was based at the National Waterways Museum and sailed on the Severn estuary. She can normally be seen at Blists Hill Museum, one of the Ironbridge Gorge Museums.

The transom stern of a Wey barge preserved at the Boat Museum.

A Yorkshire keel on the Stainforth & Keadby Canal near Crowle, Lincolnshire, c.1910.

The puffer 'Basuto' in the Boat Museum collection.

A sailing wherry on the Norfolk Broads, c.1900.

Isolated from the main waterways were the *wherries* of the rivers and broads of Norfolk and Suffolk.

Wide sailing craft were adapted for steam and diesel power. New hulls continued to be built in the traditional styles, maximising cargo capacity to raise the greatest income possible. Modern barges are more standardised in design in order to reduce boat-building costs.

Technically, narrowboats are also part of the barge family but they have been seen as something different and special, mainly because of social factors. Narrowboat families did not want their skills associated with – as they saw it – the inferior skills of the bargees. Over time their boats have come to be seen as different from barges and their way of life separated from that of others involved in carrying freight by water.

There are still fleets of barges to be seen at places such as Goole, opposite the Waterways Museum and Adventure Centre, and at Swinton, near Rotherham, where Waddingtons barges are moored between jobs.

Waddingtons barges at Swinton, South Yorkshire, in 2003.

With a hull similar to that of the sailing keels, a Waddingtons motor barge is pictured in 2003 waiting for its next job.

Two sizes of 'starvationers' near the entrance to the underground canals at Worsley on the Bridgewater Canal.

Where did narrowboats come from?

'Narrowboats' are so called because they were designed to fit the 7 feet (2.13 metres) wide locks of the 'narrow' canals. The first long-distance narrowboats worked on the Trent & Mersey Canal from the 1770s.

Before this time, the only craft around with any similarity to what became narrowboats were the *box boats* of the Bridgewater Canal. The earliest part of this waterway, which opened in the 1760s, was built specifically to bring the Duke of Bridgewater's coal to the centre of Manchester. Coal was transported within the mine on a number of narrow underground canals that eventually totalled 46 miles (74 km) and operated on three levels.

Box boats were the size of narrowboats. They remained in use until the end of carrying in the 1960s. This boat, with a 'box' sitting in it, is in the collection at the Boat Museum.

One of the smallest mine boats from the Worsley mine, on display at the Boat Museum.

Three sizes of boat were used to carry coal out of the mine in containers, which were then swung on to larger box boats and transported to Manchester. Box boats were very simply built, with straight sides of oak planks fixed by frames to cross-planked elm bottoms. The frames were so prominent on these craft that they were known as 'starvationers' because their ribs showed. The earliest box boats may have been 'long-bottomed', with the bottom planks running from bow to stern and the frames 'U'-shaped.

Narrowboats developed from these simple craft. Early illustrations show round-bilged boats, more like barges, on the Trent & Mersey. Cabins were built to accommodate the usually all-male crews and the fixtures and fittings of long-distance boats were added.

A narrowboat in London around 1820.

*Two early barge-
style narrowboats at
Worsley on the
Bridgewater Canal.*

The Trent & Mersey Canal was the first long-distance waterway built to the narrow canal gauge. It is not recorded whether the boats were designed to fit the locks or the locks were built to take boats of a size already familiar. However, James Brindley, the canal's engineer, had already worked on the Bridgewater Canal and knew all about mine boats, and so it is likely that he had the box-boat type of construction in mind when he designed the narrow locks.

There were many local influences on narrowboat design; there was no national plan. It was an age in which individual yards would build to their own specifications. On the River Trent builders of Trent keels and barges tried their hand at narrowboats and added their own touches. Similarly, a firm with no boat-building experience could set up and start to build. The early days of the canals represented a time of great experimentation. There were no handbooks to read and very little information existed for people to follow.

Construction and propulsion

Most early narrowboats were built from wood, and wooden boats continued to be built until 1960 – indeed wooden pleasure boats are still occasionally built. Iron narrowboats and barges were first built by John 'Iron Mad' Wilkinson on the River Severn in the 1780s and 1790s, but boats of this construction did not become popular until much later.

Boat construction comes in many forms, including 'composite' – built with wooden bottoms and iron sides – which became very common. Iron and steel boats required less maintenance but were more expensive and needed a certain degree of technology to build. Wooden boats could be built nearly anywhere but needed regular maintenance to replace worn side planks and bottoms. Composite boats gave the strength of iron sides but allowed the bottoms to be replaced cheaply – loaded canal boats often scraped their bottoms on the canal bed, wearing them away, and wood was easier to replace.

Right: A view into the dock at Bulls Bridge, Middlesex, where the Grand Union Canal Carrying Company maintained its fleet in the 1930s and 1940s.

Below: Repair work in progress in 1977 on a Birmingham Canal day boat showing new planks scarf-jointed in to older sections of the boat.

Top: *The blacksmiths' shed at a Walsall boatyard built from recycled boat bottoms after old boats had been broken up, 1980.*

Above: *The Severner motor narrowboat 'Oak' being reconstructed for the National Waterways Museum in 1988.*

Left: *The wooden motor boat 'Roger' returns to the water after restoration for the Rickmansworth Waterways Trust in the 1990s.*

A Birmingham day boat with a large movable mast for the horse to pull from, c.1900.

There were two distinct types within the main bulk of the narrowboat fleet: long-distance boats and day boats.

On the Birmingham Canal Navigations, day boats were in the majority. They were either 'open', with no shelter, or built with a simple cabin with a stove for an overnight stay or somewhere to rest while waiting.

Although long-distance boats usually ran on regular routes, they could cover the whole country as long as they fitted the locks. These are the typical narrowboats that people know today, with a cabin that includes a double bed, stove, cupboard, cabin table and side bed. Examples of many of these cabin boats built in wood, iron and steel can be seen all around Britain and especially at events and gatherings. The largest collection is at the Boat Museum in Ellesmere Port, where there is the opportunity to get on board and explore the family's living space and to learn something about the boat people and their way of life.

A pair of long-distance horse boats on the Grand Union Canal at Cosgrove, c.1900.

A motor and butty form a pair of boats here travelling loaded through Buckby Locks on the Grand Union Canal in the 1960s.

Right: *The best-preserved horse-boat cabin – the 'Friendship' at the Boat Museum.*

The tug 'Birchills' and the Grand Union motor boat 'Aries' at the Boat Museum.

Horse-drawn narrowboats on the Bridgewater Canal near Manchester, c.1910.

A horse-drawn Lancaster Canal barge, c.1900. A grant to restore the last one was awarded by the Heritage Lottery Fund in 2003.

Canals were designed to carry boats pulled by horses. Gradients are easy, slopes have raised brickwork for the horse to push against, and parapets are smooth and continuous for tow ropes to slip over. Boats worked singly or in pairs, usually with a single horse, though on some waterways a pair of donkeys was preferred.

Stabling was available from companies and at public houses approximately every 10 miles (16 km) along a waterway and,

A pair of horse-drawn narrowboats on the former Warwick & Birmingham Canal near Olton in about 1905.

Left: *A horse pulls a short train of 'tub boats' over the Beam Aqueduct on the Torrington or Rolle Canal. Tub boats were very small rectangular craft, often built for canals that used inclined planes instead of locks to overcome changes in the level of the ground.*

unlike the river navigations, there was a continuous towing path running alongside the canal. Some engineers would switch the path from side to side over roving or change bridges to even out the slight sideways pull of the rope and harness on the horse. This saved a horse from rubbing sore.

Other methods of propulsion were used, including drifting with the tide, sailing (as with the boats of the Chesterfield Canal) and bow hauling from the bank with gangs of men. 'Legging' was used to move a narrowboat

Stopping a horse boat on the Shropshire Union Canal at Northgate Locks, Chester, c.1910.

These photographs were taken during the making of Sight Seen Partnership's video 'Towpath Encounter', a reconstruction of the horse-drawn days on the waterways. With expert collaboration and under the guidance of the late Tom Mayo, horse boating was recorded for all to see. Sight Seen Partnership offers a range of videos on the theme of reconstructing history and can be contacted via the museums (see page 54).

This sequence shows how the canal engineers have designed the locks to ease the strain on the horse when restarting a boat from the locks. (Top left) The horse pulls a loaded boat out of the lock. (Top centre) A simple pulley system is used to halve the initial weight of the load as the boat is restarted. (Top right) One line runs to the horse and one to a fixed hook on the lock side. (Bottom left) Evidence of such fittings as this – the lock-side hook – can be found at many canal sites. (Bottom centre) The strain comes on to the pulley as the horse begins to pull. (Bottom right) As the boat gathers speed a toggle in the line meets the pulley. All the weight is transferred to the horse and the line to the hook goes slack. It will drop off the hook as the boat passes; by then the job is done.

Narrowboats with sails set on the Bridgewater Canal, c.1910.

through a tunnel where no towpath was provided; this involved lying on the boat or on boards projecting from the boat and pushing against the wall with one's legs.

Steam was used later as a means of propulsion. When steam engines became more common people tried to fit them to boats. On narrow canals it was many years before engines and boilers were made small enough for boats to accommodate them. The first successful steam narrowboats in regular service were the Grand Junction Canal boats working between London and Birmingham from 1864 until 1876, when they were sold to

A Birmingham Canal day boat working through Dudley Tunnel, c.1900. It has been legged through the narrow tunnel bores.

This official company postcard shows a Fellows, Morton & Clayton steamer and butty on the former Grand Junction Canal in 1900.

Fellows, Morton & Company (later Fellows, Morton & Clayton), who became the principal steam narrowboat owners. Compared with the thousands of horse boats in use, there was only a very small number of steamers. Even at their peak in the late Victorian period there were only around thirty in service with Fellows, Morton and a handful of other carriers.

As diesel and semi-diesel engines were introduced from 1912 onwards the steamers were taken out of service or converted to motors. The new diesels were lighter and easier to use and allowed motor boats to carry an additional 10 tons of goods more than the steamers.

The steam-powered narrowboat 'President' and its butty 'Kildare' at a national festival near Reading in 2003.

The motor boat 'Mendip', in the Boat Museum collection.

Below: *A motor boat moves away from Tyrley top lock on the Shropshire Union Canal, c.1930. The boat is pulling its butty up from the lock below on a long line as the boatwoman prepares the lock to receive it.*

As the internal combustion engine developed, many types were used in narrowboats. The earliest were sturdy semi-diesels – 'semi' in that heat has to be applied externally to help the engine start whereas a true diesel works off higher compression and internal heat. Bolinder semi-diesels were in use carrying goods on the waterways throughout the twentieth century. Fellows, Morton & Clayton fitted them to all their boats. The majority of Grand Union Canal Carrying Company boats used Russell Newberry and National diesels.

The distinctive cabin and tiller of a motor narrowboat, 'Shad', at Ellesmere Port. It is in British Waterways colours but was built for Fellows, Morton & Clayton.

Motor boats developed their own style of 'back end'. The cabin extends forward to accommodate the engine room and a counter stern with its flattened underside gives space for the propeller and stern gear to help the boat work efficiently. The 'Z'-shaped tiller was also characteristic. On butties – the unpowered partners to a motor boat, together forming 'the pair' – sterns were pointed to help water flow to the huge rudder with its long sweeping tiller. This mechanism was known as the 'helum'.

In the foreground is the 'stand' of a narrowboat. Stands are part of the structure that helps to support the hold covers of the boat. Behind is a motor narrowboat showing the colourfully painted cabin and tiller.

Pairs of Willow Wren Carrying Company boats at Braunston on the Grand Union Canal in 1969. Willow Wren took over much of the work that the nationalised fleet gave up in 1963 and at its peak had twenty-five pairs in operation.

A pair of Foxton Canal Services boats fitted for 'camping' – carrying accommodation for youth groups under the canvas hold covers; early 1970s.

Below: A tug on the Birmingham Canal with its train of loaded 'joeys' – a name relating to Joe Worsey, a local boat-builder, 1940s.

Until 1987 the compartment boat tugs and their trains of 'tom puddings' moved millions of tons of coal from the South Yorkshire pits to Goole for export.

Narrowboats and wide boats especially adapted to pull other boats have been built from the earliest days of power on water and are known as 'tugs'. The earliest steam tug was built in 1797 for trials on the Bridgewater Canal and shortly afterwards there were experiments in Scotland. A vast range of steam and later diesel-powered tugs was used on the inland waterways. In the twenty-first century the skills of working with tugs are almost entirely confined to seaports and major rivers.

The massive bows of an ex-Grand Union Canal Carrying Company pair on the left contrast with the finer lines of Fellows, Morton & Clayton boats at Braunston in 2000.

Boat-builders and types of boat

The majority of old narrowboats on the canals today come from two companies that formed the backbone of trade in the first half of the twentieth century up to nationalisation of the waterways in 1948.

Fellows, Morton & Clayton (FMC) came together as a company in 1889, though the first Fellows started carrying in 1837. The company specialised in carrying general cargoes, foodstuffs and dry goods and developed a number of set routes between warehouses such as Wolverhampton (Broad Street), Ellesmere Port and Birmingham (Fazeley Street) and locations in London. These boats also travelled widely to other destinations, and to many people a pair of 'Joshers' (after Joshua Fellows) epitomised the canals. FMC built its own craft at Saltley in Birmingham and Uxbridge in Middlesex; the company also bought some in from Yarwoods boat-building yard at Northwich in Cheshire. FMC's boats are characterised by a good 'swim' – being well shaped with a long bow and a good long stern on the butty.

The other major surviving group of boats is that of the Grand Union Canal Carrying Company. A group of ambitious businessmen came together to take advantage of government financial assistance as part of the package of measures to get

The loaded Admiral class motor 'Mountbatten' passes Dutton stop lock on the Trent & Mersey Canal in 1970.

Britain out of depression in the 1920s and 1930s. They widened and deepened their waterways and built a fleet of 356 boats, motor and butty pairs. These were ordered from a number of yards including Yarwoods, Harland & Wolfe at Woolwich in London, and Walkers at Rickmansworth, Hertfordshire, for wooden boats.

These two fleets combined to form the nationalised carrying fleet. Two new classes of narrowboat, Rivers and Admirals, were added before the fleet ceased most of its work in 1963.

Many other boat-builders' craft and other companies' boats can also be seen. Each boat-builder added his own variation to the shape of the boat.

The Admiral class butty 'Keppel' lying at Dutton between rallies, beautifully restored and maintained by British Waterways.

A Chesterfield Canal 'cuckoo' with the cabin under the stern deck at boatmen's games on the Trent. Boatmen's games were tests of boating skills and strength, especially popular on the north-eastern waterways.

Chesterfield Canal boats

The Chesterfield Canal was linked to the River Trent rather than to the rest of the narrow canal system. Its narrowboats were barge-like in character to meet the challenge of the River Trent, with its tidal wave and rough water. Their cabins were under the higher stern deck. These boats were equipped to sail and were known locally as 'cuckoos'.

Severners

Narrowboats travelled the River Severn linking the port of Gloucester to the industrial Midlands via Worcester and Stourport; locally they were known as 'long boats'. These were among the biggest narrowboats, having high sides and bows to manage the river conditions. They were built with posts (timberheads) at the front corners of the cargo space and behind the cabins to allow easy connections between strings of boats for hauling upstream by tugs or gangs of men from the bank.

Runcorn boats

Another type of large narrowboat built with timberheads, these

A Severner motor, the 'Oak', showing the large bow designed to meet the worst of river and tide.

Left: *Samuel Barlow was a well-known coal-carrying firm in the Coventry area. This picture shows the privately preserved motor boat 'Gort' in 2001.*

Below: *Henry Seddon & Sons' boats supplied their Middlewich salt works with coal. Illustrated is the 'Sweden' in private ownership in 1989.*

were also known as 'wooden headers' and were mostly used on the wide Bridgewater Canal. Six planks high, they carried up to 64 tons between a pair of boats.

Variations in use

Different companies often specialised in the cargoes they carried; for example Cowburn & Cowpar carried chemicals and Mersey Weaver transported material for the pottery industry.

The early boats included container boats. Most narrowboats were simple, open craft that could be covered by canvas to keep

A Thomas Clayton of Oldbury tank boat on the Shropshire Union Canal in the 1950s.

The horse-drawn tank boat 'Gifford', owned by the Boat Museum Society, can often be seen at rallies and events across the waterways system.

the cargo dry. Where grain or clean loose cargoes were carried, cloths would be used inside the hull to contain the cargo as well.

Some narrowboats were built as 'floats' – boats with decks on to which a cargo could be rolled or stacked. For instance, where mining companies delivered coal in tramway wagons boats could be adapted to carry the whole wagon.

The most common variations for cargo were tank boats. Claytons of Oldbury had a fleet of boats designed to carry liquids. The hull was divided by walls to hold gas oil, a by-product from gasworks used for making wood preservatives. These boats had planked decks over the cargo and were among the last boats carrying.

Variations in size

The size of boats varies from canal to canal. On the Shropshire Union Canal narrowboats 6 feet 2 inches (1.88 metres) wide were built to navigate the tub-boat locks between Wappenshall and Trench. On the Huddersfield Narrow Canal there were short narrowboats 58 feet (17.68 metres) long constructed to go through the locks on the Yorkshire side of the waterway.

Where there were no locks to negotiate and boats were on dedicated routes they could be bigger than the standard narrowboat. Length was limited by the tightest bend; width by

The wharf boat on the left overshadows the standard-size day boat 'Birchills' on the Birmingham Canals. They were photographed in 1978.

the size of bridges or narrow sections of waterway. Typical of these boats were the 'wharf boats' of the Birmingham Canal Navigations, which were up to 86 feet (26.21 metres) long and 7 feet 9 inches (2.36 metres) wide.

An open wide boat on the southern Grand Union Canal in the 1930s.

On broader canals there were classes of boats built like narrowboats but of barge size. These were known as 'bastard' boats on the Manchester, Bolton & Bury Canal, 'mules' on the Kennet & Avon Canal and simply as 'wide boats' on the Grand Union Canal.

Closely allied to narrowboats were the boats of the South Wales waterways. In the 1790s the Welsh valleys saw one of the most concentrated canal-building booms of the whole canal age. Two engineering father-and-son partnerships, the Sheasbys and the Dadfords, built four major waterways linking the coast to huge reserves of coal and iron in the Welsh valleys. Most craft were

Wide 'mules' laid up at Newbury on the Kennet & Avon Canal c. 1910.

Glamorganshire Canal craft unloading patent fuel briquettes to ships in Cardiff Docks in the 1890s.

open boats, although a few had simple cabins, and most were built double-ended so that they could travel either way by transferring the rudder from one end to the other. Swansea Canal boats were 65 feet (19.81 metres) long by 7 feet 6 inches (2.29 metres) wide, similar to narrowboat dimensions. Glamorganshire Canal and Brecon & Abergavenny Canal boats were 60 feet (18.29 metres) long by around 8 feet 6 inches (2.59 metres) wide, and Neath & Tennant Canal boats 60 feet (18.29 metres) long by 9 feet (2.74 metres) wide.

Passenger boats

The early canal entrepreneurs tried every market and responded to public demand. Once waterways linked towns, passenger services were provided. These came in two basic types. Market boats would travel regular routes carrying people and small cargoes to local centres to do business; they were not particularly speedy. Fast boats or *swift packets* carried people and the mail (packets) quickly. These reached a peak of sophistication just before the railway age began in the 1840s but never developed nationwide. Swift boats could travel at up to 14 mph (22.53 km/h) – fast for their age but only about half the speed of the first trains. Once railway lines and stations spread across the land, passenger boats began to disappear.

Maintenance craft

Further variations on hulls were shown by craft adapted for maintenance work.

Spoon dredgers were boats with a small crane and a shovel to push into mud on a canal bed. Dredgings were lifted with the spoon and tipped into the hull. This type of boat was used both for dredging the line of a canal and for cutting close into wharves and the edge of the bank, where bucket dredgers could not so

A lengthsman's boat, complete with a small cabin, hauled wherever the work took him, c.1890s.

easily reach. Spoon dredging was labour-intensive and was largely superseded by steam grab dredgers and, in the mid twentieth century, by diesel hydraulic dredgers.

Work boats comprising a variety of hulls from full-length boats to ice-breakers – carried the bricks, sand and cement for masons and bricklayers to replace lock walls and repair bridges and wharves from the water. Modern waterways have more craft specifically designed for the purpose.

Originally canals were divided into lengths, each with a lengthsman responsible for day-to-day maintenance. Lengthsmen would have small boats, often rectangular punts, to carry their tools and a supply of clay for hole stopping. The lengthsman would bow-haul his craft and work on the hedges and verges, mend leaks on the banks and carry out measures to prevent animal burrows from weakening canal structures such as embankments.

House boats with a full-length cabin would house gangs of men required for a major repair or 'stoppage'. Sleeping and cooking facilities were provided on board.

Pump boats were used to remove water from a length of canal by means of hand pumps or Archimedean screws, which they carried on board. Later steam and diesel pumps performed this work.

Ice-breakers were smaller craft, specially strengthened, that

The ice-breaking gang rock their boat as the horses pound the towpath in front; 1940s.

were used to break the ice on canals to keep trade moving. Such a boat could break ice up to 4 inches (10 cm) deep, cutting into it with a rocking action produced by the workers riding on its platform and allowing the weight of the boat and the gang to press down and break the ice. Mostly ice-breakers were used to keep a clear channel through thin ice. Once a canal was blocked by ice, trade stopped and ice-breakers could not work until the thaw set in. The majority of ice-breakers were horse-drawn but the Leeds–Liverpool Canal had steam-powered boats and in later days on wide waterways diesel-powered craft were used.

Weed-cutters were boats, usually with paddle wheels and large blades, used to cut back plants at the edges of canals or in water supply channels where their growth restricts the flow of water into a canal from a reservoir.

Committee boats. Each waterway would be inspected by its management committee, usually on an annual basis. Many companies had a special boat fitted out to entertain the group with lunch. Engineers also had their own floating offices to take them to work sites and to plan major repairs.

Pleasure and leisure craft

The share salesmen on the Trent & Mersey Canal would tempt investors with the idea of owning a gondola and taking pleasure trips on the new canal. They needed to persuade people both to invest in the waterway and to sell them the land on which to build it.

Holiday boating originated on the River Thames and the Norfolk Broads in the late Victorian period. The first holiday firm on the canal system opened in 1935 near Chester. From that time new boats were built. At first they resembled river launches

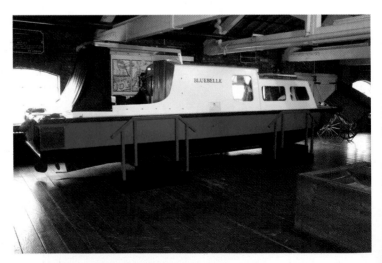

Many people's first experience of canal boating in the 1950s and 1960s was on a converted lifeboat or, as here, an army bridging pontoon – a cheap way of exploring the canals.

From Victorian times onwards there have been horse-drawn trips on the canal from Llangollen to the weir at the head of the canal. This photograph dates from about 1900.

In the early days of canals rowing boats provided taxi services on urban canals; later they became part of the leisure scene, as in this view of around 1900.

Working boats would take parties out to local beauty spots, exchanging the grime of the industrial towns for the peace of the countryside. This trip took place in about 1900.

but from the 1960s onwards they were built in steel and to the shape of narrow canal craft.

Over the years pleasure boats have developed to carry large parties, such as for the trip offered through the tunnel and caverns at Dudley from the Black Country Living Museum. Perhaps the most typical symbol of leisure on the working waterways was the Sunday-school outing. A working boat was cleared out, and wallpaper was tacked over the inside, so that a Sunday school or improvement class could travel a few miles over the local waterway. Today's canals offer many more leisure opportunities.

The unloading of a boat was almost always by hand with shovels and barrows, c.1910.

Working cargoes

Boating was an organised business and from the earliest days newspapers advertised timetables. Boats would call at warehouses, which linked with local delivery wagons and village carriers. For particularly important cargoes there were fly-boats working around the clock with two crews and constant changes of horses. This way letters and bullion, and perishable goods such as shellfish, could be moved swiftly. For more general cargoes boats travelled over fixed routes at regular times but stopped at night.

Perhaps the most advanced cargo-carrying system was that of the Shropshire Union. Across the waterways of Shropshire,

A country wharf at Aynho on the Oxford Canal in 1910. The wharf is in use today as a base for canal holidays.

A Shropshire Union Canal boat in the heart of the Black Country, c.1900.

At Ellesmere Port the Shropshire Union company had massive storage capacity for the pottery industry. Raw materials were stockpiled for delivery to the Potteries, and the finished products were brought back to await export. The Boat Museum now occupies part of this site.

A Shropshire Union fly-boat at Runcorn unloading from the Potteries, c.1890.

The Shropshire Union fleet was one link in the chain from seagoing cargoes to the factory; c. 1910.

Cheshire and the Welsh border boats moved day and night to a timetable. These services linked with craft running between Wolverhampton and Ellesmere Port, from where in turn there were links to Liverpool and Manchester, and there were also links from the Black Country to London. A series of warehouses along the canals acted as local depots at which goods could be left for shipment. A fleet of boats, 450 strong at its height, was in service until 1921.

This system was subsidised by its parent company, the London & North Western Railway (LNWR). As the canal penetrated the territory of rival railway companies, it offered the LNWR a relatively cheap way of competing with the Great Western and Cambrian Railways.

Milk – a cargo for Cadbury's Knighton factory on the Shropshire Union Canal in the 1930s.

The site seen in this view of c.1900 is now part of the Black Country Living Museum at Dudley and is still full of canal interest, although the limekilns finished work many years ago.

The piles of limestone tower over narrow-boats on the Caldon Canal as they load up in about 1910.

Working boats on the Oxford Canal near Banbury in 1963.

Blue Line continued to transport coal to London until 1970, when the last contract finished. An empty pair waits at Braunston on its way back to the collieries near Coventry to reload.

Samuel Barlow's 'Grace', loading near Coventry. Barlow was a 'number one' boatman (which means he owned his boat) who started his coal-carrying firm in the late nineteenth century. The company sold out to Blue Line in 1962 and moved over to road haulage.

A Willow Wren pair in Buckby Locks. Started in 1952, the company finally ceased trading in 1970 after a spirited fight to keep business on the canals.

There were also many boats that operated on the canals as if they were part of a conveyor belt moving primary materials from mines and quarries to factories. Coal, iron ore, stone and clay were needed in vast amounts by industry. Many factories had been built beside canals when the waterways served as the major transport network.

Canals continued in use until the old factories were replaced by new ones located alongside the newer rail or road connections. The last major traffics disappeared in the 1960s, after two hundred years of narrowboat carrying, as oil replaced coal as fuel in the last canal-side factories.

Boats today

There are still barges carrying cargoes such as sand, gravel, stone, fuel oil and steel products on the inland waterways, with the greatest concentration of boats trading on those of the north-east – principally the Aire & Calder Navigation. Other cargoes include domestic waste on the Thames. New services are always under review and in 2003 two new craft began to carry gravel on the Grand Union Canal near London.

Experiments with waste traffic on the River Lee and proposals for gravel traffic on the River Severn may lead to new freight business. Encouraging waterborne freight is government policy and grant aid is available for new craft, work on wharves and unloading equipment. There are still small flows of coal in narrowboats, mostly for domestic use. Most variations of narrowboat can still be seen on the canals.

On both wide and narrow waterways a dedicated few continue to run boats in a traditional way, keeping alive the spirit of the commercial waterways. The continual tightening of regulations will change the nature of waterway trade but groups such as the Commercial Boat Operators' Association are determined to continue.

Working boats are kept by individuals and in museums. Magazines such as *Waterways World*, *Canal and Riverboat* and *Canal Boat* detail rallies and events in which boats participate.

A modern barge moves down to load over the side from a seagoing ship in Goole Docks in 2003.

Above: 'Clover' and 'Fazeley' descend the reopened Caen Hill Locks on the Kennet & Avon Canal en route to filming with the BBC in 1996.

Left: 'Lupin' leaves Stoke Bruerne Bottom Lock in 1998 with a load of bagged domestic coal to sell over the side on the way to London.

Below: 'Jubilee' approaching Bugbrooke on the Grand Union Canal with coal early in 2002 – one of many cargoes keeping carrying alive through the Commercial Boat Operators' Association.

'Shad', on loan from the Boat Museum, unloads coal at Stoke Bruerne in 2002.

There is a major event each Easter at the Boat Museum, Ellesmere Port, Cheshire, at which twenty or more narrowboats gather. Horse-drawn boats are much less common but the Horseboating Society can give details of events and trips. Stoke Bruerne in Northamptonshire is a particularly good place to see boats; there is usually a narrowboat at the Canal Museum and all types of boats pass by. Both the National Waterways Museum at Gloucester and the Boat Museum have boats open to the public.

One of the great benefits of being a waterways enthusiast is that you can live the dream and own your own narrowboat. The magazines offer a vast range of boats for sale every month, from traditional full-length ex-working boats to smaller modern hulls. Groups such as the Historic Narrow Boat Owners Club welcome new members with or without boats and can provide a wealth of knowledge and experience.

Privately preserved narrowboats from all over England meet at the Boat Museum, Easter 1999.

Stoke Bruerne in horse-drawn days. The mill on the left now houses the Canal Museum.

People who are interested in getting afloat without owning a boat can join societies such as the Wooden Canal Boat Trust, the Shropshire Union Fly-boat Trust, the Friends of *President*, the Boat Museum Society and the Friends of the Working Boats, all of which offer the opportunity to help restore and maintain craft while getting the chance to work with a narrowboat as it journeys round Britain. Joining such a society is perhaps the best way to explore the inland waterways and understand the details of locks and engineering structures that relate to working craft.

There is almost always a cabin open for view at the Boat Museum.

Above left: *British Waterways' 'Keppel' and 'Lindsay' en route to a rally.*

Above right: *The Shropshire Union Fly-boat Restoration Society's 'Saturn' – the last in a class of hundreds of boats – represents an opportunity to help restore and run a working boat.*

The privately owned 'Darley' on the Shropshire Union Canal in 2000.

Members of the Friends of the Working Boats prepare British Waterways' 'Atlas' and 'Leo' for filming.

Above and left: *The Humber Keel and Sloop Society's 'Comrade' and 'Amy Howson' preserve the skills of sailing craft on the Humber estuary.*

There are also groups working with wide craft, especially sailing boats. The Humber Keel and Sloop Society and the Norfolk Wherry Trust maintain working boats. There are groups associated with the spritsail barges of the Thames and there are gatherings of Leeds–Liverpool Canal boats each year.

It is important to keep boats working so that the techniques needed to operate boats in local conditions are understood, recorded and passed on. The sight of a well-handled working pair of narrowboats or a sailing wherry brings the waterways alive, and to see a loaded barge at work reminds us why the inland waterways were built in the first place.

Further reading

Some of the books listed below are not widely available in bookshops or are out of print. Try public libraries, second-hand booksellers, bookstalls at events, the columns of canal magazines and the Internet.

General

De Salis, H. R. *Bradshaw's Canals and Navigable Rivers*. Reprinted by David & Charles, 1969. The opening pages neatly encapsulate a description of the working waterways and their boats.

Lansdell, Avril. *Canal Arts and Crafts*. Shire, second edition 2004.

Lewery, Tony. *Flowers Afloat*. David & Charles, 1996. A comprehensive and richly illustrated book on the decoration of boats.

Paget-Tomlinson, Edward. *The Illustrated History of Canal and River Navigations*. Sheffield Academic Press, 1994. A comprehensive reference work covering all aspects of the inland waterways.

Pratt, Derek. *London's Canals*. Shire, fourth edition 2004.

Smith, Peter L. *Discovering Canals in Britain*. Shire, fourth edition 1993, reprinted 1997.

Ware, Michael E. *Canals and Waterways*. Shire, 1987; reprinted 2003.

Boats and boat people

Chaplin, Tom. *The Narrow Boat Book*. Whittet Books, 1981. A comprehensive review of narrow canal craft.

Paget-Tomlinson, Edward. *Britain's Canal and River Craft*. Moorland Publishing, 1979. A good general book on all inland waterway craft.

Rolt, Tom. *Narrow Boat*. Eyre Methuen, 1944. A fascinating snapshot of life on the canals in 1939–40.

Stewart, Sheila. *Ramlin Rose*. Oxford University Press, 1993. A beautifully written and researched novel based on the recorded lives of Oxford Canal boating families in the early twentieth century.

Ware, Michael. *Narrowboats at Work*. Moorland Publishing, 1989. A good photographic survey.

Wilson, Robert. Various titles. Robert Wilson Publications. First published in the 1970s and reprinting from 2002, this range of small books provides individual fleet and company histories for most major carrying fleets, broad and narrow.

Museums

Black Country Living Museum, Tipton Road, Dudley, West Midlands DY1 4SQ. Telephone: 0121 557 9643. Website: www.bclm.co.uk (Has a working boat dock with canal boats including wharf boats. A good canal site.)

The Boat Museum, South Pier Road, Ellesmere Port, South Wirral, Cheshire CH65 4FW. Telephone: 0151 355 5017. Website: www.boatmuseum.org.uk (The major national collection of inland waterway craft.)

The Canal Museum, Stoke Bruerne, Towcester, Northamptonshire NN12 7SE. Telephone: 01604 862229. (A great spot to watch today's narrowboats on the Grand Union Canal.)

London Canal Museum, 12–13 New Wharf Road, King's Cross, London N1 9RT. Telephone: 020 7713 0836. Website: www.canalmuseum.org.uk (Has temporary exhibitions and a good website.)

The Museum of the Broads, The Staithe, Stalham, Norfolk NR12 9BZ. Telephone: 01692 581681. Website: www.whiteswan.u-net.com/museum (Has boats and exhibits relating to the Norfolk Broads.)

National Waterways Museum, Llanthony Warehouse, The Docks, Gloucester GL1 2EH. Telephone: 01452 318200. Website: www.nwm.org.uk (Outlines the history of the waterways and has a collection of canal craft on display.)

River and Rowing Museum, Mill Meadows, Henley-on-Thames, Oxfordshire RG9 1BF. Telephone: 01491 415600. Website: www.rrm.co.uk (Has boats and exhibits relating to the River Thames and Henley.)

Waterways Museum and Adventure Centre, Dutch Riverside, Goole, East Yorkshire DN14 5TB. Telephone: 01405 768730. Website: www.waterwaysmuseumandadventurecentre.co.uk (Presents the history of the north-east waterways and is a great place to see working barges.)

Windermere Steam Boat Museum, Rayrigg Road, Windermere, Cumbria LA23 1BN. Telephone: 01539 445565. Website: www.steamboat.co.uk (Has an inclusive collection of pleasure, leisure and ferry boats used on Lake Windermere.)

Societies

Friends of the Working Boats. Website: www.workingboats.com (Aims to keep alive the skills of working boats through training.)

Humber Keel and Sloop Preservation Society. Website: www.humberships.org.uk (Preserves and sails the traditional craft of the north-east's inland waterways.)

The Norfolk Wherry Trust. Telephone: 01603 505815. (Has one of the last trading wherries, built in 1898 for transport on the Norfolk Broads and restored for pleasure sailing.)

Wooden Canal Boat Society, c/o 5 Oaken Clough Terrace, Lime Hurst, Ashton-under-Lyne OL7 9NY. Telephone: 0161 330 2315. Website: www.wcbs.org.uk (This collection of important craft includes 'Hazel' (1914) and 'Queen' (1917). The earliest craft is the 'Lilith' of 1901. The society is based at Portland Basin Museum in Ashton-under-Lyne, open Tuesday–Sunday. Volunteers are on site most Sundays.)

Websites

www.canaljunction.com – a wide-ranging site.

www.jim-shead.co.uk – covers various subjects and includes an illustrated boat guide.

www.cboa.org.uk – the official site of the Commercial Boat Operators' Association.

www.nb-president.org.uk – all about the steam narrowboat *President* and has links to steam boat sites all over the United Kingdom.

www.narrowboat.igw.com – website of the Narrow Boat Trust.

www.hnboc.org.uk – website of the Historic Narrow Boat Owners Club, which aims to encourage the preservation, restoration and use of working narrowboats.

www.british-waterways.com – includes maps and information.

www.saturnrestoration.org.uk – dedicated to the restoration of a Shropshire Union fly-boat.

www.horseboating.org.uk – promotes horse boating and includes photographs, information and links to operators.

The National Waterways Museum's horse boat 'Northwich' and the Boat Museum Society's tank boat 'Gifford' pass during filming on the Worcester & Birmingham Canal.

Index